BILINGUAL PRESCHOOL

English-Spanish

by
Patricia Gómez and Diana I. Shelton
Music by Sara Jordan

Produced and Published by
Sara Jordan Publishing
a division of

ISBN 978-1-55386-072-3

Acknowledgments / Reconocimientos

Lyricist - Patricia Gómez

Lyricist for Songs 10 and 11 - Diana I. Shelton

Editors - Robert Gaiero, Diana I. Shelton, María Manrique

Composer, Producer - Sara Jordan

Music Co-producer, Arranger, Engineer - Mark Shannon

Male Singer - Ricky Franco

Female Singer - Shantall Young

Illustrations - Jessica Jordan-Brough

Cover Design - Campbell Creative Services

Interior Layout - Darryl Taylor

Digitally Recorded and Mixed by Mark Shannon,
The TreeFort, Toronto, Ontario.

For further information contact:

Jordan Music Productions Inc.
M.P.O. Box 490
Niagara Falls, NY
U.S.A. 14302-0490

Jordan Music Productions Inc.
Station M, Box 160
Toronto, Ontario
Canada, M6S 4T3

Internet: http://www.sara-jordan.com
E-mail: sjordan@sara-jordan.com
Telephone: 1-800-567-7733

To David, my son,
who every day
teaches me something new.

Para David, mi hijo,
quien todos los días
me enseña algo nuevo.

The translation of these bilingual songs is close in most cases; however, in some verses, similar words and arrangement of the words were used to obtain better musical results.

We acknowledge the financial support of the Government of Canada through the Book Publishing Industry Development Program (BPIDP) for our publishing activities.

Contents/Contenido

Hints for Teachers and Parents

Bilingual Preschool: English-Spanish provides teachers, parents and early learners with an innovative approach to second language learning.

These songs, which combine curriculum-based content with fun and movement, offer an attractive and easy-to-use format that facilitates learning in both Spanish and English.

This is a great way to provide bilingual learning while providing the 60 minutes of daily structured physical activity recommended by the National Association of Sports and Physical Education.

These bilingual songs integrate skill development through exciting rhythms and melodies that also provide a real-world context for cultural understanding.

Whether hopping, jumping, throwing the bean bag, playing "Follow the Leader" or "Eye Spy", these age-appropriate songs and games help early learners to develop and refine motor skills. The 11 bonus instrumental tracks included on the audio CD add to the fun as students use them for special performances.

Enjoy! *¡Disfrútalo!*

Here are a few ways to foster cooperative learning while building on students' basic gross motor skills, allowing them to learn more complex tasks:

- Have students practice hopping, skipping, jumping forward, backward, to the left, to the right, balancing on one foot and catching the bean bag, while listening to *Follow the Leader*, *Movin' and Groovin* and *Bean Bag Toss*.
- Encourage imaginative play and teach sequencing with *Follow the Leader* by having your children waddle like a duck, hop like a frog, etc.
- Enjoy "circle time" while teaching colors, shapes and sizes by having students sing *Eye Spy*.
- Have "finger play" fun with *Hickory Dickory Dock* while children learn to tell time
- Address phonemic awareness by having students find matching words with *The Rhyme Game*
- Allow students to take a more active part, while "feeling the rhythm" of the songs, by using rhythm instruments such as: tambourines, drums, shakers, maracas and rhythm sticks.

Please visit our websites to learn more about our educational resources. While you're there, sign-up for our free online newsletter to have free songs, activities and lesson ideas delivered right to your e-mail inbox.

www.SongsThatTeach.com

www.Aprendecantando.com

Nº 1

Let's All Sing Together
Cantemos todos juntos

Let's all sing together
Join in everyone.
Singing in two languages
is lots of fun.

If we learn and if we laugh
the fun never ends.
If we speak two languages
we will have more friends.

Cantemos todos juntos
vengan todos ya.
Cantar en dos idiomas
te divertirá.

Si aprendemos y reímos
es divertido.
Si hablamos dos idiomas
tendremos más amigos.

If we speak two languages
we will have more friends.

Si hablamos dos idiomas
tendremos más amigos.

Nº 2

The Rhyme Game
El juego de la rima

chorus/*coro:*

Play the rhyme game.
Sing along!
Play the rhyme game.
Play along!

Juega a rimar.
¡A cantar!
Juega a rimar.
¡A jugar!

Hey, _______!
It's your turn.
What should we name the cat?
How about Pete?
How about Pat?
Choose the name that rhymes
with 'at'. _____!

¡Oye, _________!
Es tu turno.
¿Qué nombre le ponemos al gato?
¿Qué tal Pepito?
¿Qué tal Renato?
Escoje el nombre que rime
con 'ato'. ¡____!

chorus/*coro*:

Hey, _______!
It's your turn.
What should we name the lion?
How about Ben?
How about Brian?
Choose the name that rhymes
with 'ion'. _____!

¡Oye, _________!
Es tu turno.
¿Qué nombre le ponemos al león?
¿Qué tal Ramiro?
¿Qué tal Ramón?
Escoje el nombre que rime
con 'ón'. ¡____!

chorus/*coro*:

Hey, ________!
It's your turn.
What should we name the hen?
How about June?
How about Jen?
Choose the name that rhymes
with 'en'. _____!

¡Oye, _________!
Es tu turno.
¿Qué nombre le ponemos a la gallina?
¿Qué tal Mariana?
¿Qué tal Josefina?
Escoje el nombre que rime
con 'ina'. ¡____!

chorus/*coro*:

Hey, _______!
It's your turn.
What should we name the bunny?
How about Zack?
How about Sonny?
Choose the name that rhymes
with 'unny'. _____!

¡Oye, _________!
Es tu turno.
¿Qué nombre le ponemos al conejito?
¿Qué tal Paco?
¿Qué tal Benito?
Escoje el nombre que rime
con 'ito'. ¡____!

chorus/*coro:*

Tips and Ideas for Performing the Rhyme Game

The Rhyme Game is intended to be used as an interactive song. A different child can be addressed at the beginning of each verse. This child, of course, will respond with the answer at the end of the verse.

You may find it easiest to have the teacher (or leader) sing the verses (with the exception of the answer) and have the children sing the choruses.

By using the music accompaniment tracks, this song can be taken one step further, with the teacher substituting many different rhyming words into the lesson.

Sugerencias e ideas para interpretar el juego de la rima

El juego de la rima está hecho para ser usado de manera interactiva. Un niño diferente puede ser nombrado al comienzo de cada verso y al final de éste tendrá que dar la respuesta.

Puede encontrar más fácil hacer que el (la) maestro(a) (o líder) cante los versos (con excepción de la respuesta) y que los niños canten los coros.

El (la) maestro(a) puede llevar esta canción mucho más lejos, usando las pistas musicales y remplazando diferentes palabras que rimen.

Nº 3

Follow the Leader
Sigue al líder

chorus/*coro:*

Follow the leader.
Pay attention all the time.
Follow the leader.
You will do fine.

Sigue al líder.
Presta mucha atención.
Sigue al líder.
Tú lo harás bien.

I can gallop like a horse.
Let's all gallop like a horse.
Puedo galopar como un caballo.
Galopemos como un caballo.

All day long.
Todo el día.

I can waddle like a duck.
Let's all waddle like a duck.
Puedo caminar como un pato.
Caminemos como un pato.

I can gallop like a horse.
Let’s all gallop like a horse.
Puedo galopar como un caballo.
Galopemos como un caballo.

All day long.
Todo el día.

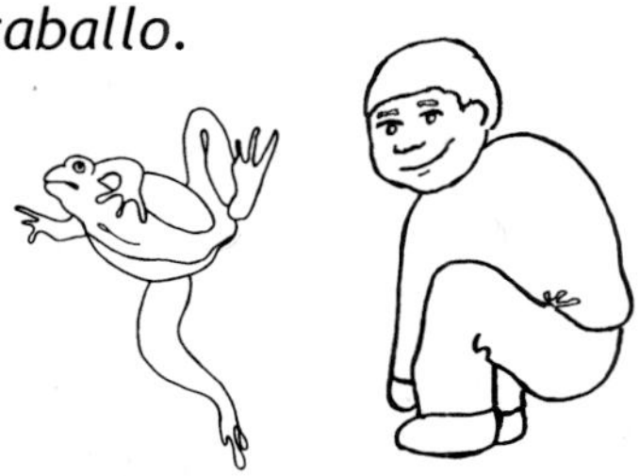

I can hop like a frog.
Let’s all hop like a frog.
Puedo brincar como una rana.
Brinquemos como una rana.

I can waddle like a duck.
Let’s all waddle like a duck.
Puedo caminar como un pato
Caminemos como un pato.

I can gallop like a horse.
Let’s all gallop like a horse.
Puedo galopar como un caballo.
Galopemos como un caballo.

All day long.
Todo el día.

I can fly like a bird.
Let's all fly like a bird.
Puedo volar como un pájaro.
Volemos como un pájaro.

I can hop like a frog.
Let's all hop like a frog.
Puedo brincar como una rana.
Brinquemos como una rana.

I can waddle like a duck.
Let's all waddle like a duck.
Puedo caminar como un pato
Caminemos como un pato.

I can gallop like a horse.
Let's all gallop like a horse.
Puedo galopar como un caballo.
Galopemos como un caballo.

All day long.
Todo el día.

chorus/*coro*:

Follow the leader.
Pay attention all the time.
Follow the leader.
You will do fine.

Sigue al líder.
Presta mucha atención.
Sigue al líder.
Tú lo harás bien.

Nº 4

Mind Your Manners
Cuida tus modales

chorus/*coro:*

Mind your manners, every day.
Be polite in many ways.
Whether it's at home or school.
Kids who have good manners rule!

En la casa o en la escuela,
tus modales debes cuidar.
Sé educado en todas partes.
¡Tener buenos modales es genial!

'Please' and 'Thank you'.
'Excuse me' and 'Good bye'.
We can have good manners.
It's easy if we try.

'Por favor' y 'Gracias'.
'Disculpe' y 'Adiós'.
Podemos tener buenos modales.
Es fácil si lo intentamos.

chorus/*coro:*

Say ‘Hello’ and ‘How are you?’
to everyone you greet.
We use manners every day
with everyone we meet.

Si con alguien te encuentras,
un saludo debes dar.
Usa tus buenos modales;
diciendo “Hola. ¿Cómo está?”

chorus/*coro:*

'Excuse me' is polite
if you do something abrupt.
When someone's speaking, listen.
Do not interrupt.

Si algo brusco haces,
'Disculpa' debes decir.
Cuando alguien habla, escucha.
No debes interrumpir.

chorus/*coro:*

Nº 5

Groovin' and Movin'
Ritmo y movimiento

chorus/*coro*:

Turn your head from
side to side;
to the left,
to the right.

Shake your hands.
Jump up and down.
We're the liveliest
kids around.

Gira
la cabeza;
a la izquierda,
a la derecha.

Agita
las manos y salta.
Somos los chicos
más animados.

Take two skips to the left.
Take two skips to the right.
Take two skips to the front.
Take two skips back again.

Dos brincos a la izquierda.
Dos brincos a la derecha.
Dos brincos al frente.
Dos brincos hacia atrás.

chorus/coro:

Shake your hands to the left.
Shake your hands to the right.
Shake your hands to the front.
Shake your hands down again.

Agita las manos a la izquierda.
Agita las manos a la derecha.
Agita las manos al frente.
Agita las manos abajo otra vez.

chorus/coro:

Hop and shake to the left.
Hop and shake to the right.
Hop and shake to the front.
Hop and shake back again.

Brinca y agita a la izquierda.
Brinca y agita a la derecha.
Brinca y agita al frente.
Brinca y agita hacia atrás.

chorus/coro:

Nº 6

The Silly Man
El hombre chiflado

I saw a silly man
walking down the street.
The silly man had a pet
walking at his feet.

Guess which pet
was at his feet?
Walking with the silly man
going down the street?

[roar] A Lion!

Caminando por la calle
vi a un hombre chiflado.
Tenía una mascota
caminando al lado.

¿Cuál mascota crees
que iba al lado?
¿Caminando por la calle
con el hombre chiflado?

[rugir] ¡Un león!

chorus/*coro:*

When we grow up and
we act silly too
the animals we take for walks
won't be from the zoo.

Cats will meow
and dogs will bark
and everyone will feel safe
when we walk through the park.

Cuando crezcamos y
aun como niños seamos,
el animal que paseemos del
zoológico no será.

Los gatos maullarán
y los perros ladrarán
paseando por el parque
todos seguros se sentirán.

I saw a silly man
walking down the street.
The silly man had a pet
walking at his feet.

Guess which pet
was at his feet?
Walking with the silly man
going down the street?

[ee-ee-ee] A monkey

Caminando por la calle
vi a un hombre chiflado.
Tenía una mascota
caminando al lado.

¿Cuál mascota crees
que iba al lado?
¿Caminando por la calle
con el hombre chiflado?

[i-i-i] ¡Un mono!

chorus/*coro:*

I saw a silly man
walking down the street.
The silly man had a pet
walking at his feet.

Guess which pet
was at his feet?
Walking with the silly man
going down the street?

[howl] A wolf!

Caminando por la calle
vi a un hombre chiflado.
Tenía una mascota
caminando al lado.

¿Cuál mascota crees
que iba al lado?
¿Caminando por la calle
con el hombre chiflado?

[aullar] ¡Un lobo!

chorus/*coro:*

Nº 7

I Spy / *Veo, veo*

I spy with my little eye
something that is yellow.

Veo, veo. ¿Qué es lo que ves?
Una cosa, que amarilla es.

chorus/*coro:*

It might be square or round.
It might be tall or small.

It might be light or heavy.
Let me point to what I see.

Puede ser cuadrada o redonda.
Puede ser alta o chica.

Puede ser liviana o pesada.
Déjame mostrarte lo que veo.

(student points to the item)

I spy with my little eye
something that is blue.

Veo, veo. ¿Qué es lo que ves?
Una cosa, que azul es.

chorus/*coro:*

(student points to the item)

I spy with my little eye
something that is green.

Veo, veo. ¿Qué es lo que ves?
Una cosa, que verde es.

chorus/*coro:*

(student points to the item)

I spy with my little eye
something in the sky.

Veo, veo. ¿Qué es lo que ves?
Una cosa que en el cielo está.

So many colors, way up high.
The rainbow's beauty in the sky.
So much beauty I can see.
Nature's gift to you and me.

Muchos colores allá arriba,
el arco iris en el cielo está.
Tanta belleza puedo ver
que la naturaleza nos da.

We recommend having children sit in a circle for this song with items (of various colors and descriptions) that you have collected, placed in the middle of the circle. Students can then discuss both the color and description of the items they have chosen.

Para esta canción, recomendamos que los niños se sienten en círculo. En el centro de éste, ubique varios objetos que usted haya reunido y sobre los cuales los alumnos tengan la oportunidad de discutir sobre sus colores y características.

How to Use This Song

Once students know the song by heart, you may wish to use the music accompaniment tracks on the CD in order to teach other colors. Students can also be asked to identify whether items are square, round, tall, small, light or heavy.

Cómo usar esta canción

Una vez aprendida la canción, puede usar las pistas musicales que contiene el CD, para enseñar a sus alumnos otros colores. Pídales también que identifiquen si los objetos son cuadrados, redondos, altos, bajos, livianos o pesados.

Other colors which could be used:
Otros colores que pueden ser usados:

red	rojo
purple	morado
orange	naranja / anaranjado
pink	rosado
black	negro
grey	gris
brown	marrón
beige	beige (beis)
white	blanco

Nº 8

Hickory Dickory Dock

chorus/*coro* 2x:

Hickory Dickory, Dickory, Dock
Hickory Dickory, Dickory, Dock
El ratón corrió al reloj.
The mouse ran up the clock.

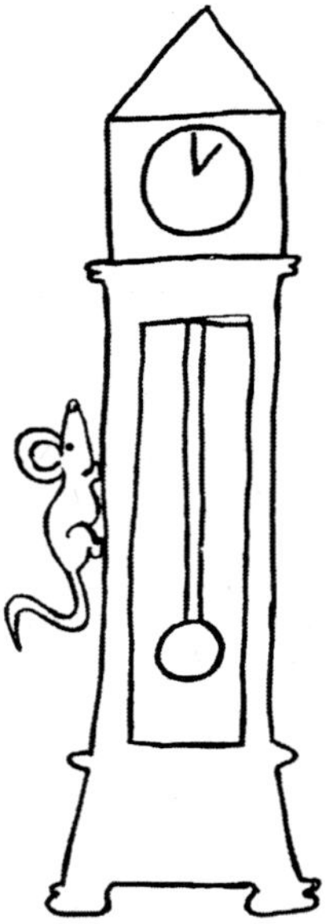

El reloj dio la una.
The clock struck one
Vamos a divertirnos.
Let's have some fun.

El reloj dio las dos.
The clock struck two.
¡No hay queso para ti!
No cheese for you!

El reloj dio las tres.
The clock struck three.
¡La hora del té!
Time for some tea!

El reloj dio las cuatro.
The clock struck four.
Él al suelo cayó.
He fell to the floor.

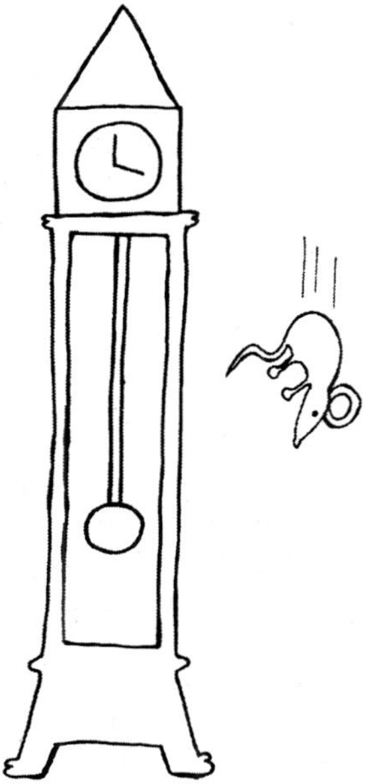

El reloj dio las cinco.
The clock struck five.
De nariz saltó.
What a nose dive.

El reloj dio las seis.
The clock struck six.
Su cabeza era dura.
His skull was thick.

chorus/*coro 2x:*

El reloj dio las siete.
The clock struck seven.
Gritó de repente.
The mouse started yellin'.

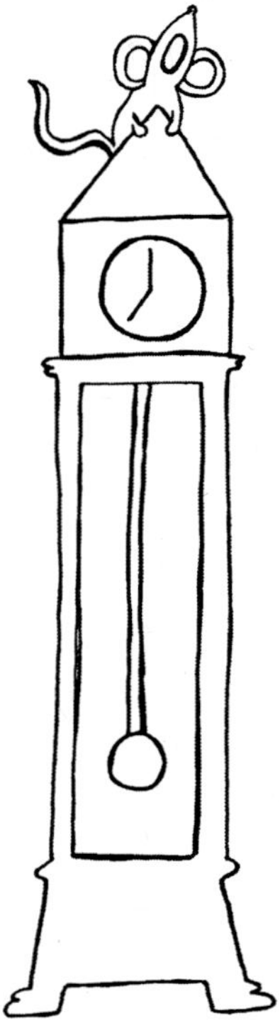

El reloj dio las ocho.
The clock struck eight.
Pensó que iba tarde.
He thought he was late.

El reloj dio las nueve.
The clock struck nine.
Es casi la hora.
It's almost time.

El reloj dio las diez.
The clock struck ten.
Él cayó otra vez.
He fell down again.

El reloj dio las once.
The clock struck eleven.
Aprendió la lección.
He learned his lesson.

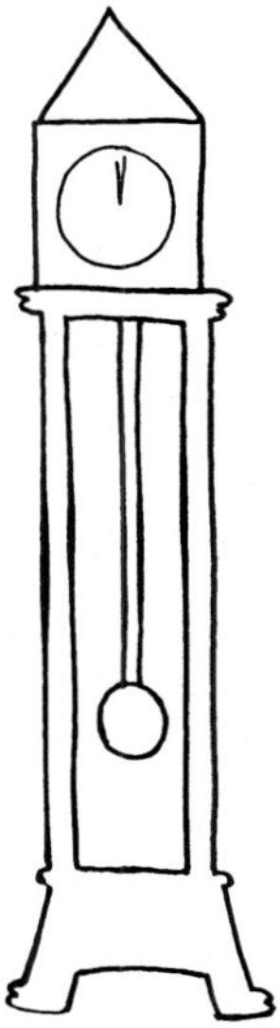

El reloj dio las doce.
The clock struck twelve.
Él brincó al estante.
He jumped to the shelf.

chorus/*coro 2x:*

Nº 9

Bean Bag Toss
Lanza la bolsa

Throw your bean bag
with your right hand.
Catch your bean bag
with the left.

Throw your bean bag
way up high.
Catch your bag.
Twirl around.

Throw your bean bag
with the left hand.
Catch your bean bag
with the right.

Throw your bean bag
way up high.
Catch your bag.
Crouch to the ground.

Lanza la bolsa
con la derecha.
Tómala
con la izquierda.

Lanza la bolsa
bien arriba.
Tómala
y da la vuelta.

Lanza la bolsa
con la izquierda.
Tómala
con la derecha.

Lanza la bolsa
bien arriba.
Tómala
y agáchate.

chorus/*coro:*

Bean bags. So much fun.
Throw it up. Twirl around.
Bean bags. So much fun.
Catch your bag. Jump up and down.

Las bolsas son diversión.
Lánzala y da la vuelta.
Las bolsas son diversión.
Tómala y luego salta.

Put your bean bag
on your head.
Walk around
don't let it fall.

Try to balance
like an airplane.
Keep your arms
spread out wide.

Keep that bean bag
on your head.
Don't let it fall
to the ground.

Keep your head
really steady.
Take your bean bag
for a ride.

Ponte la bolsa
en la cabeza.
Camina
y que no caiga.

Balancéate
como un avión.
Mantén los brazos
bien abiertos.

Mantén la bolsa
en la cabeza.
No dejes que
se caiga.

Mantén la cabeza
bien firme.
Lleva la bolsa
dando saltos.

chorus/*coro 2x:*

Nº 10

A Bike Race
Una carrera de ciclistas

Chorus/*coro:*

first *primero*
second *segundo*
third *tercero*
Bikes come racing round the bend.
En la bici compiten.*

fourth *cuarto*
fifth *quinto*
sixth *sexto*
Racing faster to the end.
Al final veloz corren.

Sing twice: seventh *séptimo*
eighth *octavo*
nineth and tenth place.
noveno y décimo lugar.

Eyes peeled on the finish line
to see who comes first this time.
Todos mirando al final
para ver al primero en llegar.

**bici= short form for bicicleta* (bicycle)

one, *uno*	1
I was first.	1st
Fui el primero.	1°
two, dos	2
I was second.	2nd
Fui el segundo.	2°
three, *tres*	3
I was third.	3rd
Fui el tercero.	3°
four, *cuatro*	4
I was fourth.	4th
Fui el cuarto.	4°

chorus/*coro:*

five, *cinco*	5
I was fifth.	5th
Fui el quinto.	5°
six, *seis*	6
I was sixth.	6th
Fui el sexto.	6°
seven, *siete*	*7*
I was seventh.	7th
Fui el séptimo.	7°
eight, *ocho*	*8*
I was eighth.	8th
Fui el octavo.	8°

chorus/*coro:*

nine, *nueve* 9
I was nineth. 9th
Fui el noveno. 9°

ten, *diez* 10
I was tenth. 10th
Fui el décimo. 10°

Hey. We're done.
Now it's time
to have some rest.

¡Sí, lo hicimos!
¡Vamos ya
a descansar!

chorus/*coro:*

Nº 11

Going Places
Ir a los lugares

I am going... I'm going
going to the movies. I'm going.
You are going... You're going
to meet me there. You're going.

Yo voy... Yo voy
voy al cinema.
Tú vas... Tú vas
a verme allá. Tú vas.

He is going... He's going
going to the café. He's going.
She is going... She's going
to meet him there. She's going.

Él va... Él va
va al café de la esquina.
Ella va... Ella va
a verlo allá. Ella va.

We are going...
going to the concert.
They are going...
to meet us there.

We're going
We're going.
They're going
They're going.

Nosotros vamos...
vamos al concierto.
Ellos van...
a vernos allá.

(Nosotros) vamos
Ellos van
Ellos van.

You are going...
to be together.
They are going...
to have fun there.

You're going.
You're going.
They're going
They're going.

Vosotras vais...
a reunirse con ellas.
Ellas van...
a verse allá.

(Vosotras) vais
Ellas van
Ellas van.

Español para principiantes

Great for beginners! Learn the alphabet, farm animals, counting, family members, parts of the body, days of the week, colors, fruit, opposites and shapes in Spanish. Perfect for students of all ages who want to learn a new language.

Spanish for Kids: Beginning Lessons Resource Book

Reproducible, black-line, thematic lessons and exercises in Spanish, based on *Español para principiantes*, teach the alphabet, numbers, days of the week, opposites, colors, family members, body parts and much more! Lessons are enhanced with information about Hispanic culture. 64 pages. Beginner level.

Canciones temáticas para aprender idiomas

This album of phenomenal singing teaches common expressions, clothing, meals, modes of transportation, weather, parts of the body, pets and rooms in the house. There is even a song teaching the correct use of prepositions! This is an interesting and useful album for beginning Spanish speakers of any age.

Spanish for Kids: Thematic Lessons Resource Book

Reproducible, black-line thematic lessons and exercises in Spanish, based on *Canciones temáticas*, teach common expressions, salutations, time, modes of transportation, pets, prepositions and much more! Lessons are enhanced with information on Hispanic culture. 64 pages. Beginner level.

Math Resource/Lyrics Books with Audio CDs

Songs, group activities and reproducible exercises teach addition, subtraction, multiplication and division. The upbeat songs make learning memorable. The reproducible exercises reinforce what has been learned in the songs while also incorporating strands of the Common Core Math Curriculum. IN ENGLISH, FRENCH OR SPANISH

Singing Sight Words Volumes 1-4

This collection of fun songs builds a solid foundation for all beginning readers. By incorporating Dolch sight words into memorable and catchy melodies, early readers are quickly able to recognize the more common and basic words found in age-appropriate literature. IN ENGLISH

Learning Sight Words Volumes 1-4 Resource Books

This four-part series of 64 page, reproducible, resource/activity books teaches students 300 of the most commonly used sight words. The words are presented in order of frequency and are based on the 200 most frequently used service words compiled by Edward William Dolch, Ph.D., and the related list of 95 high-frequency nouns. It is estimated that 50-75% of all words used in school books, library books, newspapers and magazines are included in the Dolch Basic Sight Vocabulary. This series can be used independently or in tandem with the audio/book series Singing Sight Words. IN ENGLISH

Funky Phonics®: Learn to Read Volumes 1-4

Blending the best in educational research and practice, Sara Jordan's four part series provides students with the strategies needed to decode words through rhyming, blending and segmenting. Teachers and parents love the lessons while children will find the catchy, toe-tapping tunes fun.
IN ENGLISH

Funky Phonics®: Learn to Read Volumes 1-4 Resource Books

Reproducible, black-line, thematic lessons and exercises, based on the *Funky Phonics®: Learn to Read* audio series, is a structured program providing students with the strategies needed to decode words. Teachers, parents and beginning readers love the lessons, hands on activities and reproducible worksheets.
IN ENGLISH